People of the Middle Ages

Minstrel

Melinda Lilly

Original illustrations by Cheryl Goettemoeller

Rourke

Publishing LLC
Vero Beach, Florida 32964

www.rourkepublishing.com

For Scott

To My Darling Daughters, Laurena and Jade - C.G

PICTURE CREDITS: Page 6, "Meister Heinrich Frauenlob,"(Cod. Pal. Germ. 848, fol. 399r) from the *Codex Manesse*, courtesy of the University of Heidelberg; Page 9, Page detail, St. Martial Codex, Ms. LAT. 1118, fol. 114r, Cliché Bibliothèque nationale de France, Paris; Page 14, "Der Kanzler," (Cod. Pal. Germ. 848, fol. 423v) from the *Codex Manesse*, courtesy of the University of Heidelberg; Page 21, "Herr Alram von Gresten," (Cod. Pal. Germ. 848, fol. 311r) from the *Codex Manesse*, courtesy of the University of Heidelberg; Page 22, Ms. FR. 12473, fol. 110v, Cliché Bibliothèque nationale de France, Paris; Page 25, "Office of the Dead," from *Book of Hours, Llangattock Hours*, unknown, about 1450–1460, 26.4 x 18.4 cm., The J. Paul Getty Museum, Los Angeles; Page 29, "Initial L' from the Bute Psalter, Bute Master (illuminator) and Workshop of the Passion Master (illuminator), about 1270–1280, third quarter, 14th century, 16.9 x 11.9 cm., The J. Paul Getty Museum, Los Angeles. Original art on the cover and pages 5, 10, 13, 17, 18, and 26 is by Cheryl Goettemoeller.

Cover illustration: A minstrel entertains a small group of people. In the Middle Ages (years 500 to 1500) people listened to minstrels for fun and to get news.

Editor: Frank Sloan

Cover design by Nicola Stratford

Library of Congress Cataloging-in-Publication Data

Lilly, Melinda
   Minstrel / Melinda Lilly
    p. cm. — (People of the middle ages)
   Includes bibliographical references and index.
  Summary: An introduction to the music and life of a minstrel in Europe in the Middle Ages.
   ISBN 1-58952-228-1
    1. Minstrels—Juvenile literature. 2. Music—500-1400—History and criticism—Juvenile literature. [1. Minstrels. 2. Music—History and criticism. 3. Middle Ages. 4. Civilization, Medieval.] I. Title.

ML182 .L55 2002   2001056511
782.4'3'0940902—dc21

Printed in the USA

CG/CG

Table of Contents

What's a Minstrel?

Do you like to make up songs? Are you a poet who likes to show it? If you lived during the Middle Ages (from the year 500 to 1500) you could have been a minstrel. These men and women made up poems and songs. Many of them also sang. People of Europe listened to them for fun and to get news.

A woman minstrel sings as a man minstrel plays an instrument called a cornett.

Bringing and Singing the News

There are no newspapers. If there were, few could read them. How do people know if King Harold is kind? Did Princess Blanche win the battle? It is your job, as a minstrel, to comment on the happenings of the day.

The audience gasps as you sing an epic, a story of a great hero. Your love poetry makes everyone sigh. Leave them laughing with a **sirvente** song about a silly prince they think they know.

While musicians play below, a Swiss minstrel sings. The lady and her shield are in the picture to show the subject of the minstrel's song—he sings of her.

7

What Do You Want to Be When You Grow Up?

When you speak, songs dance off your tongue. However, you are the child of a shepherd. Can you become a minstrel? Yes! Unlike most careers of the time, your father's job does not matter. With your talent, you'll soon be performing at castles!

It's easier for men than women, though. All women minstrels come from good families. A peasant woman who sings, dances, and juggles well could be an entertainer called a **joglaresa**.

A joglaresa of the 900s sings, dances, and plays bells. An example of early sheet music can be seen below her feet.

Studying Music

You've just turned eight. Time to choose your future career. You want to be a **troubadour**. Troubadours were minstrels in southern France during the years 1000 to 1300. How do you become one? Have your parents ask a troubadour to teach you to play music, sing, and compose songs.

If you are a boy, you might attend school. Mind your lessons. You learn to play an instrument and sing church songs. Perhaps you will learn to read and write music. Sheet music is a new invention.

A boy practices his lute while his music teacher listens.

11

Instruments of the Middle Ages

"Play a song!" the people cry. You strum your lute and sing of lost love. When they want to dance, your bagpipe helps them step lively.

At church, you hear the **organetto**. It is pumped like an accordion and played like a piano.

It's dinnertime at the castle. Call people to the table with a blast from your double pipe. After the meal, you sing and play a new instrument—the **lira de braccio**. It's the mother of the violin.

Upper left: lute, center: organetto, upper right: bagpipe, lower left: lira de braccio, lower right: double pipe

Minstrels

Every country in Europe has minstrels. Southern France is famous for its troubadours. In Germany, you are called a **minnesinger**. As an English minstrel, you thrill the crowd with tales of Robin Hood.

You are paid well. You might get 500 coins or a gold robe trimmed with fur. Your host knows that if you are not treated fairly, at the next castle you will sing about his cheapness.

A minnesinger and two musicians of the 1300s are shown in this songbook of the Middle Ages.

15

From Castle to Castle

During the summer, you can travel from place to place along the old Roman roads. Men minstrels often choose to move around. Women usually sing at one castle.

Hitch a ride in a peddler's cart. Ride a donkey or horse. Sling your lira de braccio across your back and head off across the countryside!

A minstrel sets off on his travels with his horse and lira de braccio.

Minstrel Festival

You practice your songs as you arrive at the fair. After greeting the other minstrels, you enter the music festival. At last, it is your turn. "I wonder where you hide your heart," you sing. Musicians play. Dancers twirl. Jugglers and acrobats amaze.

The local lord announces that you have won! People cheer as he gives you the prize— one hundred coins!

A minstrel sings at a fair of the Middle Ages.

Love, Sweet Love

More than other minstrels, troubadours like to sing about love. Some songs claim that fine love makes a man noble. Others cry about impossible love. These romantic ideas are new to the Middle Ages.

You swear your love to a lady by kneeling in front of her. She cradles your clasped hands. You promise to serve and defend her. If she accepts, she places a ring on your finger. Then she kisses you!

A minstrel sings to the lady he loves. The word "amor" is French for love.

Trobairitz

If you are a woman minstrel, you are a **trobairitz**. The name means a woman who invents songs. After dinner at the castle, you begin to sing to another minstrel. You flirt with him using words and melody. He sings back.

The two of you make up your song while you sing it. You tease each other about the silly things men and women do. Everyone smiles at your song, called a tenson.

Castelloza, a famous trobairitz of the 1200s

Harmony

When you go to church, you hear a different type of music. People sing in a style called **plainsong**. Everyone sings the same notes.

During the Middle Ages, people in church start singing in harmony. You sing one set of notes. Other people sing different notes that sound good with yours. Since that time, most songs use harmony.

Nuns and monks sing. This picture is from a book of the Middle Ages. All books of the Middle Ages were made by hand. They are called illuminated manuscripts.

War!

The year is 1208. Pope Innocent III, the head of the Church, calls for war. He wants to kill the **Cathars** of southern France. They are members of a different religion.

War begins the next year. Your life as a troubadour changes forever. Armies of the Church attack your country. Whether you are a Cathar or not, you may be killed. In 1229, the war ends. The Cathars are dead. Castles where you have sung are overthrown.

Knights attack a castle.

End of the Troubadours

The Church's war, called a **Crusade**, brings an end to troubadours. All music has to be church music. You can't sing about ladies and knights. Your poems are now about holy people of the Church, such as the Virgin Mary.

However, your songs do not die out. Minstrels of other places sing them. Love songs on the radio today have their beginnings in the songs of the minstrels of southern France!

This page is from a holy book of the Middle Ages. It shows the writing of the time and a musician inside the letter "L".

Exultabunt sancti in gloria: leta
buntur in cubilibus suis.
Exultationes dei in gutture eorum: et
gladii ancipites in manibus eorum.
Ad faciendam uindictam in na
tionibus: increpationes in populis.
Ad alligandos reges eorum in compe
dibus: et nobiles eorum in manicas ferreas
Ut faciant in eis iudicium conscrip
tum: gloria hec est omnibus sanctis eius
Laudate dominum in sanctis
eius: laudate eum in fir
mamento uirtutis eius
Laudate eum in uirtutibus eius: lau
date eum secundum multitudinem mag

Dates to Remember

476	Last Roman emperor overthrown (Romulus Augustulus)
500	Beginning of the Middle Ages
About 1000	Harmony begins to appear in western music.
About 1035	Guido D'Arezzo invents an early form of sheet music
1100–1200s	Heyday of troubadours in what is now southern France
About 1200	Castelloza born
1208	Pope Innocent III calls for a Crusade against the Cathars.
1229	Peace of Paris signed. This treaty officially ends the Crusade against the Cathars, although there are battles waged until the year 1255.
1500	End of the Middle Ages
About 1525	Invention of the violin

Glossary

Cathars (KATH arz) — members of a Christian religion of the Middle Ages other than Catholic

Crusade (kroo SAYD) — a war of the Middle Ages in which Christian soldiers attacked people of another religion

joglaresa (johg lah RES ah) — a woman performer of the Middle Ages

lira de braccio (LEE rah deh BRA cho) — violin-type instrument that came before the violin

minnesinger (MIN neh sing er) — a Germanic minstrel of the Middle Ages

organetto (OR gan et toe) — an instrument of the Middle Ages

plainsong (PLANE song) — early Christian songs in which singers sing together

sirvente (SIR vent) — a poem or song that makes fun of something or someone

troubadour (TROO buh dore) — a poet of the Middle Ages in southern France

trobairitz (TROO buh ritz) —a woman troubadour

Index

Further Reading

Czarnota, Lorna MacDonald. *Medieval Tales That Kids Can Read and Tell.* August House Pub., 2000.

MacDonald, Fiona. *The Middle Ages.* Facts on File, Inc., 1998

Shuter, Jane. *The Middle Ages.* Heinemann Library, 2001.

Websites to Visit

Art of Illuminated Manuscripts of the Middle Ages:
   www.bnf.fr/enluminures/aaccueil.htm

Instruments of the Middle Ages and Renaissance:
   www.s-hamilton.k12.ia.us/antiqua/instrumt.html

Explore a castle:
   www.nationalgeographic.com/castles/enter.html

About the Author

Melinda Lilly is the author of several children's books. Some of her past jobs have included editing children's books, teaching pre-school, and working as a reporter for *Time* magazine. She is the author of *Around The World With Food & Spices* also from Rourke.

32